Oliver CROMWELL

DAVID DOWNING

Heinemann
LIBRARY

www.heinemann.co.uk/library
Visit our website to find out more information about **Heinemann Library** books.

To order:
☎ Phone 44 (0) 1865 888066
▤ Send a fax to 44 (0) 1865 314091
▭ Visit the Heinemann Bookshop at www.heinemann.co.uk/library to browse our catalogue and order online.

First published in Great Britain by Heinemann Library, Halley Court, Jordan Hill, Oxford OX2 8EJ, part of Harcourt Education.

Heinemann is a registered trademark of Harcourt Education Ltd.

Produced for Heinemann by Discovery Books Ltd
Editorial: Helen Dwyer, Nicole Irving, Andrew Solway and Jennifer Tubbs
Design: Barry Dwyer
Illustrations: Stefan Chabluk
Picture research: Rachel Tisdale
Production: Séverine Ribierre

Originated by Dot Gradations
Printed and bound in China by South China Printing Company

ISBN 0 431 13884 2
07 06 05 04 03
10 9 8 7 6 5 4 3 2 1

British Library Cataloguing in Publication Data
Downing, David
  Oliver Cromwell. – (Leading lives)
  941'.064'092

A full catalogue record for this book is available from the British Library.

Acknowledgements
The publishers would like to thank the following for permission to reproduce photographs: Corbis: p. **55** (Angelo Hornak); Bridgeman Art Library: pp. **6** (Chequers, Buckinghamshire), **33** (Harris Museum and Art Gallery, Preston), **53** (Bolton Museum and Art Gallery); Hulton Archive: pp. **8**, **10**, **18**, **32**, **35**, **36**, **40**, **42**, **48**, **54**; Mary Evans Picture Library: pp. **5**, **7**, **14**, **15**, **17**, **20**, **22**, **27**, **34**, **37**, **44**, **47**, **51**; Peter Newark: pp. **12**, **24**, **28**, **30**, **39**.

Cover photograph of of a portrait of Oliver Cromwell reproduced with permission of Peter Newark.

Every effort has been made to contact copyright holders of any material reproduced in this book. Any omissions will be rectified in subsequent printings if notice is given to the publishers.

Contents

1 A controversial life	4
2 Childhood and youth	6
3 Gentleman farmer	10
4 Member of Parliament	15
5 Horse soldier	20
6 The New Model Army	25
Map of major battles of the English Civil War	25
7 The fall of the king	29
8 Ireland and Scotland	36
9 The Commonwealth	40
10 Lord Protector	45
11 Legacy	52
Timeline	56
Key people of Cromwell's time	58
Further reading and other resources	60
Glossary	61
Index	64

Any words appearing in the text in bold, **like this**, are explained in the Glossary.

A controversial life

Imagine the following men:

A young Member of **Parliament**, so passionate about his religious and political beliefs that he was often criticized for the violence of his language. He believed that the king wished to cut back the powers of Parliament, and that Parliament should be prepared to fight a **civil war** to preserve its powers.

A military leader of great personal courage, with a talent for both organization and battlefield tactics. He was the only man of his time to realize, and act upon, two important facts – that men fought better and harder for beliefs than for money, and that when it came to leadership, the ability to command soldiers was much more important than social rank.

A member of the **gentry** who was forced to choose between the **establishment** and the soldiers who had fought under him, and chose the soldiers.

A political leader who organized the execution of a king in the name of one Parliament, and was later offered the kingship by another.

A man who fought a war to preserve Parliament's power, and then used his victorious army to overthrow a series of Parliaments.

A loving husband and father and a caring friend.

Oliver Cromwell was all these men. In his own century he was admired for his bravery but condemned for serving the wrong cause. In the 18th century he was considered a complete hypocrite. Historians of the 19th century thought

▲ *Oliver Cromwell, as painted by Robert Walker in the late 1640s. This painting hangs in London's National Portrait Gallery.*

him a great **constitutional** reformer, while those of the 20th century saw him as a bewildering mixture of all these things.

Few men in history have had such a mixed press, such a variety of reputations. So which was the essential Oliver Cromwell? Where did he come from, and how did he come by the extreme religious and political ideals that motivated his later life? How did the MP become the general? How did he win a civil war, and then lose the peace? What turned the fighter for Parliament into a destroyer of Parliaments? How did the killer of a king become almost a king himself?

Childhood and youth

Oliver at the age of two. The fact that such a portrait was painted is proof of his family's prosperity.

Oliver Cromwell was born in the small East Anglian market town of Huntingdon on 25 April 1599, the fifth of Robert and Elizabeth Cromwell's ten children. Seven of these were daughters – three older than Oliver, four younger – and all but the eldest reached adulthood. Oliver's brothers were not so lucky: his older brother Henry died young, probably before Oliver reached his teens, and his younger brother Robert died as a baby.

A member of the gentry

His mother's family, the Stewards, had lived in East Anglia for many generations. His father's family, which had both **Norman** and Welsh roots, had been granted former church lands around Huntingdon by Henry VIII in the mid-16th century. By the time of Oliver's birth his parents were country landowners, not particularly wealthy, but a great deal better off than the vast mass of the population, who owned no land at all. And in one respect they were better favoured than others with more wealth: the Cromwell family was related to many of the most powerful names in the land.

They belonged to the **gentry**, the social class below royalty and the **aristocracy**, and above the **yeomanry** of small farmers and craftsmen. Robert Cromwell was a local **Justice of the Peace** and a Westminster MP. In a speech many years later Oliver would sum up his birthright thus: 'I was by birth a gentleman, living neither in any height nor yet in obscurity.'

Games and God

Oliver went to school at the Huntingdon Free Grammar School, some hundred metres along the High Street from the family home. Little is known for certain about Oliver's early life

▲ Cromwell's mother Elizabeth, who came from the East Anglian Steward family.

but it is clear that he was not an outstanding student. He seems from an early age to have developed in two opposing directions. On the one hand he greatly enjoyed physical pursuits, on the other he liked to think, to meditate, about things. Inside him, the future religious reformer and the future military leader were competing for attention, as they would throughout his life.

In religious matters he was probably deeply influenced by Sir Thomas Beard, a well-known **Puritan** writer who first arrived to teach at the school when Oliver was five. The God in whom Thomas Beard believed was a constant presence at everyone's shoulder, guiding and judging, bringing victory to the righteous and defeat to the ungodly. This was the God Oliver would grow up to believe in.

Taking charge

Sir Thomas Beard probably had an important say in Oliver's choice of college. Oliver went to Sidney Sussex College in Cambridge, which at the time was considered a hotbed of Puritanism. Oliver, however, was still enjoying the less puritanical things of life, and he seems, from many accounts, to have spent as much time gambling, playing games and chasing women as he spent learning Latin. This period came suddenly to an end after 14 months, when news arrived of his father's death. Eighteen-year-old Oliver, as the family's only surviving male, had to take charge of the family estate.

He returned to Huntingdon, at least for a while. In the early 17th century it was usual for important figures in a local community to learn some law, and it seems likely that Oliver spent a year or so studying at one of the London **Inns of Court**, most probably Lincoln's Inn.

Puritanism and the 'Godly reformation'

In the early and mid-16th century a movement to reform the **Roman Catholic** Church led to the **Reformation**: the establishment of a new branch of Christianity called **Protestantism** in many parts of northern and western Europe. Over the century that followed, many of the new Protestants attempted to introduce more reforms. They were called Puritans.

The Puritans wished to make Puritan churches even less Catholic than they already were, by getting rid of the remaining rituals, and by encouraging spontaneity and a more direct relationship between individuals and God. They wanted less supervision from appointed authorities like the bishops, and more independent preachers. They tried to live their lives according to basic Christian principles, and believed this would lead others to follow their example. Eventually, they believed, the whole society would be transformed by this **'Godly reformation'**.

During this period he met and fell in love with Elizabeth Bourchier, the daughter of a prosperous fur and leather merchant.

After their marriage at St Giles's Church in London's Cripplegate on 22 August 1620, Oliver took his new bride home to Huntingdon. For most of the next 20 years he would make a living from the land and help to raise a family.

Gentleman farmer

Oliver and Elizabeth Cromwell seem to have suited one another very well. More than 30 years after their marriage he was still writing to tell her 'thou art dearer to me than any other creature.' From the beginning, Elizabeth was happy to play the role of the traditional wife, taking care of children and the home while her husband took care of business. She gave birth to seven children – Robert, Oliver, Bridget, Richard, Henry, Elizabeth and James – between 1621 and 1631, and another two – Mary and Frances – in 1637 and 1638.

During his twenties Cromwell seems to have enjoyed the usual pursuits of a country landowner: hunting, fishing, riding and caring for horses. He was a fiery character with strong opinions, but he also liked a good joke, and was fond of singing and dancing. Happily married with a growing family and no real money worries, he had every reason to consider himself a fortunate man.

▶ Oliver's wife Elizabeth. They married in 1620, and were together until his death almost forty years later. She outlived him by seven years, dying in 1665.

Changes

The years from 1628 to 1631 brought great changes in Cromwell's life. In 1628 he was elected to represent Huntingdon in the **Parliament** summoned by King Charles I. Arriving in Westminster, he found that nine of his cousins had also been elected. He made his first speech in February 1629, and like most of his fellow MPs grew increasingly annoyed by the king's high-handed attitude towards Parliament (see page 12). But when Charles dismissed Parliament a few months later, Cromwell, like all his fellow MPs, had no choice but to return home.

FOR DETAILS ON KEY PEOPLE OF CROMWELL'S TIME, SEE PAGE 58.

Back in Huntingdon, he was soon in trouble. When a decision was taken to replace the elected local government with officials appointed for life by the king, Cromwell's objections were loud and strong. So strong in fact that in 1630 he was called before the king's Privy Council (the ruling council of government appointed by the king) and forced to apologize for his rudeness. With Huntingdon now run by the king's supporters, Cromwell knew that he had no chance of being re-elected as the town's MP. He sold most of his property in and around the town, and moved his family to a rented farm in nearby St Ives.

The Cromwells had come down in the world. For the next five years they would be living below the imaginary line which separated the **gentry** from the **yeomanry**, and it seems unlikely that Oliver Cromwell ever forgot the experience. For the rest of his life he would have a foot in both camps.

Seeing the light

During these years Cromwell learnt a great deal about the England he lived in, about Parliament and king, gentry and yeomanry. He also seems to have suffered something of a

King and Parliament

The disputes between King Charles I and his various Parliaments had two obvious strands, the religious and the political. Where religion was concerned most **Protestants**, and particularly **Puritans** like Cromwell, were keen to continue with the **Reformation** of the 16th century, to rid their religion of its remaining **Roman Catholic** elements. The king, on the other hand, along with his Catholic wife and the Catholic-leaning Archbishop Laud, was trying to roll back the Reformation and reintroduce things like universal prayer books, which symbolized the **established** church's role as a vital **intermediary** between individuals and God.

FOR DETAILS ON KEY PEOPLE OF CROMWELL'S TIME, SEE PAGE 58.

During the same period, the dominant group of Puritans in Parliament, led by John Pym, was trying to increase Parliament's powers. If they succeeded in this, they could push forward their programme of religious reform and reduce the burden of the king's taxes on London's growing business class, to which most of them belonged. The king, of course, opposed an increase in Parliament's powers. He was determined to keep the powers he had. This was partly because he wanted to push forward his own religious programme, and partly because he really believed that God had given him these powers, that he had a **divine right to rule**.

Parliament's crucial advantage was its control over taxation. As long as the king had money enough to pay for his plans he had no need to summon Parliament, but the moment he faced a financial crisis – as he did over his wars with the Scots in 1639 and 1640 – he needed Parliament to grant him money.

◄ John Pym, who led the Puritan group in Parliament until his death in 1643.

personal crisis, a series of descents into depression which ended with a profound religious conversion. 'Blessed be His name for shining upon so dark a heart as mine!' he wrote in 1638; 'you know what my manner of life hath been. Oh, I have lived in and loved darkness, and hated the light. I was a chief, the chief of sinners.'

This conversion set Cromwell on a path he would never abandon. From this point forward the **Puritan** religion would be his guiding light in all matters, both religious and political.

'Lord of the Fens'

In 1636 the family had another, more welcome, reversal of fortunes. They inherited estates in and around Ely from Cromwell's uncle Sir Thomas Steward, and found themselves back among the ranks of the gentry. By this time, however, Cromwell had developed a strong sense of social justice.

It is hard to say where this sense came from – whether he was born with it, whether it grew out of his Puritan faith, his experiences in Parliament or his years among the yeomanry. But by the end of the 1630s it was a central part of who he was. For Cromwell, social justice was not about creating equality. It was about people accepting their responsibilities in life, the lower classes giving the upper classes the respect they deserved, and the upper classes helping out the lower classes.

In 1636 a big row developed over the draining of the Fens, the low-lying areas north of Ely that flooded in winter. Draining the Fens would provide more land to grow the food the country needed, but the people who made their living from hunting and fishing in the Fens would lose their livelihoods. Cromwell championed the cause of the Fenlanders, and earned himself the half-admiring, half-sarcastic nickname 'Lord of the Fens' as a result.

Back to Parliament

In May 1639 Cromwell suffered a personal tragedy – his eldest son Robert, away at school, suddenly died at the age of 17 as a result of either accident or illness. This loss, Cromwell later wrote, was like a 'dagger to my heart'.

Meanwhile, the king had made the disastrous mistake of trying to impose his religious programme – in the form of a new prayer book – on the Scots. The Scots preferred war to Charles' religion, and invaded northern England. Desperately in need of money, Charles had no choice but to summon a new Parliament. In the spring of 1640, men like Cromwell, now elected as an MP for Cambridge, poured into Parliament, eager to cut the king down to size, eager to begin the **'Godly reformation'** of England.

◀ *King Charles I, as seen around 1635 by Anthony van Dyck. This portrait, which was painted before Parliament began its serious challenge to the monarchy, shows Charles sure of himself and his right to rule.*

Member of Parliament

Soon after Charles I summoned **Parliament** in the spring of 1640, Oliver Cromwell enjoyed his 41st birthday. By the standards of the time, he was now well into middle age, but in good health. He was 1.78 metres tall, well-built, with blue eyes and a prominent nose in a rugged face. According to one of his parliamentary opponents, his voice was 'sharp and irritable'; both friends and foes were struck by his outspokenness and his fiery temper. His dress was as plain as his speech, but John Hampden, a prominent Parliamentary leader, was not fooled. 'That slovenly fellow' he told a fellow MP, would, if it came to 'a breach with the King', be 'one of the greatest men in England'.

FOR DETAILS ON KEY PEOPLE OF CROMWELL'S TIME, SEE PAGE 58.

A torrent of reforms

In the spring of 1640 Cromwell was not among the first rank of Parliamentary leaders, but he was a prominent member of the second rank. Over the next two years the arguments between Parliament and king escalated towards **civil war**.

▶ John Hampden, whose challenge to the King's extension of Ship Money (a tax traditionally paid by people in coastal towns in return for naval protection) was an early step on the road to civil war.

Charles dismissed the first Parliament of 1640 (the Short Parliament) because it refused to give him any money unless he agreed to reforms, but he was forced to summon another later that year. This parliament (the Long Parliament, which sat until 1653) set out on a programme of wide-reaching political and religious reforms. It decided that Parliaments were to sit for a minimum of 50 days at least every three years, and that this particular Parliament could not be dismissed without its own agreement. Ship Money and other royal taxes were abolished, and the king was forced to execute or imprison some of his leading ministers.

The reforms amounted to a severe cutting back of the king's powers, and Cromwell was repeatedly in the thick of things. He was a frequent speaker, often introduced **bills** of reform, and sat on important committees, including several concerned with reform of the church. He often lost his temper, and gave the impression of a man in a desperate hurry. The chance had come to begin the **Godly reformation** of England, and he was determined not to waste it.

The Grand Remonstrance

By the autumn of 1641 many MPs thought that the balance between Parliament's power and the king's was now about right. Around an equal number, however, were intent on pushing for further reforms, and Cromwell was among them. Public opinion seemed to be swinging in favour of the first, conservative group, until the outbreak of a **Roman Catholic** rebellion in Ireland. The (mostly false) reporting of terrible atrocities committed by Irish Catholics against Irish **Protestants** frightened English Protestants, and the king's liking for a more Catholic church now told against him. The

▶ *A Royalist playing card makes fun of Parliamentary commanders Cromwell and Fairfax.*

Cromwell pypeth unto Fairfax.

radicals suddenly found themselves able to push forward new reforms.

They delivered the Grand Remonstrance to the king, a list of 204 occasions on which they said he had acted illegally, and they demanded a **veto** over his future appointment of ministers. The Grand Remonstrance was passed, but, rather to Cromwell's surprise, by only 11 votes. He told a friend that if it had been rejected, he 'would have sold all he had the next morning, and never seen England more'.

The king and his opponents now had almost equal power and support. Both sides believed they were right, and that God was on their side. Neither saw any reason to give way. When, in December 1641, Parliament passed a bill taking control of the armed forces away from the king, it cut the ground from under his feet. Without an army, the king could not enforce his will, and he had no choice but to respond. On 4 January 1642 the king invaded the **House of Commons** with his personal troops. His aim was to arrest

17

▲ *The King's invasion of the House of Commons on 4 January 1642, as drawn by Wenceslaus Hollar.*

the five most prominent MPs ranged against him – Pym, Hampden, Denzil Holles, William Strode and Sir Arthur Haslerig – but they had already escaped down the River Thames to the City of London.

Slide into war

This move made it clear that the king's dispute with the ruling group in Parliament could no longer be resolved peacefully. Through the first six months of 1642 the two sides continued to bombard each other with suggestions and demands, but they also prepared for war.

On the Parliamentary side Cromwell's importance grew rapidly. He demanded that Parliament should seriously consider putting the kingdom on a full military alert, and was prominent among those who put up money for the raising of troops, supposedly for action against the Irish rebels, but in fact for the Parliamentary cause. In July he organized the raising of volunteer companies in his own East Anglian area, and in mid-August he led an ambush on the Great North Road, boldly intercepting a shipment of **silver plate** on its way from Cambridge University to the king.

On 22 August 1642, Charles declared war on Parliament. A few days later, Cromwell assembled his own force of cavalry from the counties of Huntingdonshire and Cambridgeshire. Within a month it was on its way to join the main force of the Parliamentary army, led by the Earl of Essex.

5 Horse soldier

To locate Edgehill, see the map on page 25.

In the autumn of 1642 the king's army won the first major battle of the war at Edgehill, but his commanders failed to follow up the victory, and fighting was halted for the winter. Almost all of the **gentry** supported the king, while the **yeomanry** and business classes generally sided with **Parliament**. The king's greater number of trained soldiers offered him hope of a speedy victory, but Parliament's greater ability to raise money gave it the long-term advantage.

Into battle

Cromwell and his troop arrived late on the Edgehill battlefield and saw little action. He spent most of the rest of the year in

Parliament, arguing frequently and forcibly to continue the war. He was involved in the decision to form an Eastern Association army in East Anglia, and was appointed one of its four colonels under the overall leadership of the Earl of Manchester. In February 1643 his own cavalry troop was upgraded to a regiment (an army unit led by a colonel). Its men became known as the **Ironsides**, because in battle they proved so hard to break or divide.

◀ *Cromwell on horseback. He had ridden since his childhood, and would prove one of the greatest cavalry leaders in English history.*

Right from the start, Cromwell was determined to employ men who wanted to fight for the same reasons he did, to create a better, more godly England. He was not interested in soldiers motivated by fear or greed, or in members of the gentry who thought of war as an exciting game. 'I had rather have a plain russet-coated captain that knows what he fights for and loves what he knows than what you call a gentleman and is nothing else.' he said. 'If you choose godly honest men to be captains of horse, honest men will follow them.'

Cavaliers and Roundheads

As the **civil war** got under way each side gave the other a nickname. The Parliamentary forces called the Royalists 'Cavaliers', from the Spanish *caballeros*, in order to mock their supposed pro-foreign and pro-Catholic sympathies. The Royalists called the Parliamentary forces 'Roundheads', for following the fashion among London **apprentices** for cutting their hair short as a sign of their rebellion against the king's authority.

Cromwell insisted on strict discipline among his troops because he knew disciplined troops were more effective in battle. Throughout 1643 – which, generally, was a bad year for the Parliamentary forces – his horse soldiers distinguished themselves and their commander. In May a fierce charge scattered a strong Royalist force near Grantham, and a daring uphill attack at the siege of Gainsborough in July was equally successful. When the sudden arrival of a strong Royalist army forced him into a retreat, this too was handled with skill. In October, Cromwell teamed up with the Yorkshire Parliamentarian Thomas Fairfax, and their joint force won a convincing victory at Winceby in Lincolnshire. During this battle Cromwell had two horses shot from under him.

FOR DETAILS ON KEY PEOPLE OF CROMWELL'S TIME, SEE PAGE 58.

FOR DETAILS ON KEY PEOPLE OF CROMWELL'S TIME, SEE PAGE 58.

Needing the Scots

Cromwell spent much of the autumn at home in Ely, where a romance was blossoming between Major Henry Ireton – his future right-hand man – and Cromwell's serious-minded eldest daughter Bridget. As winter arrived he moved back to London, where Parliament considered what it should do next. The king's forces had won many minor victories, and Parliament had lost its two leading **Puritan** MPs, John Hampden (in battle) and John Pym (to cancer).

In desperation Parliament signed a Solemn League and Covenant with the Scots in November 1643. By this agreement, the Scots promised military assistance to Parliament in return for money and a loosely-worded Parliamentary promise that the established (officially recognized) Church of England would become **Presbyterian**. Men like Cromwell, who considered Presbyterianism almost as restrictive as Catholicism, had no intention of honouring such a promise, but they were prepared to argue with the Scots after the king had been defeated.

▲ Henry Ireton, who married Cromwell's daughter Bridget, and remained his closest ally until his early death in 1651.

Marston Moor

In January 1644 Cromwell was promoted to Lieutenant-General. He was now the Earl of Manchester's second-in-command, and the sole commander of the Eastern

Presbyterians and Independents

The **Puritans** – those who wished to continue the reformation of the established church – were divided into two groups: Presbyterians and **Independents**. Neither wanted bishops appointed from above, but the Presbyterians favoured electing elders or 'Presbyters' to run the church, while the Independents wanted to do away with church authorities altogether. The latter's rejection of central control created space for the growth of small Independent religious groups, like the **Quakers** and **Fifth Monarchists**.

The Presbyterians were dominant in Scotland, but in England opinions were more evenly divided. The more conservative sections of society tended to support Presbyterianism, with its built-in respect for authority. Those interested in social reform and revolution found much more to admire in the unpredictable, anti-authoritarian spirit of the Independents.

Association's cavalry. The following month he was voted onto Parliament's new Committee of Both Kingdoms, which would be responsible for the day-to-day running of the war. Alone on the Parliamentary side, Cromwell was an important politician and also a military leader.

In early spring he took to horse once more, leading a series of raids against the king's strongholds, including Charles' capital, Oxford. Other Parliamentary leaders seemed less eager to conduct the war with the same energy, and in the early spring of 1644 Cromwell began to wonder whether some of his fellow-commanders were as interested in victory as he was.

During these weeks news reached him that his second son Oliver had died of smallpox (an infectious disease), but he had little time for grief: the war was now reaching towards a climax. In early summer, a Parliamentarian army led by Thomas Fairfax, aided by the Scots, laid siege to a Royalist army in York. Meanwhile two other armies – the Royalists commanded by the king's nephew Prince Rupert, and the Parliamentarians led by Manchester and Cromwell – marched to the aid of their allies. On 2 July all these armies came together in one terrible battle on Marston Moor, the biggest battle ever fought in the British Isles.

To LOCATE MARSTON MOOR, SEE THE MAP ON PAGE 25.

The Royalist cavalry charged straight through their opponents and as usual kept going straight on. Cromwell's cavalry showed the discipline needed to reform its ranks and charge again. Cromwell himself, though injured in the neck, led his men to a victory that turned the tide of the war.

◄ The Royalist cavalry commander Prince Rupert, as seen in a 1643 engraving.

The New Model Army

After the victory at Marston Moor in July 1644 the Parliamentary side's divisions became increasingly bitter. The **Presbyterians** were now happy with the **status quo**, and wanted to do a deal with the defeated king which would leave him with considerable powers. The **Independents** were hungry for more changes. Some of them, like Cromwell, still hoped for an agreement with the king, while others were prepared to get rid of the monarchy altogether.

The Self-Denying Ordinance

This division of opinion affected the progress of the war. The Presbyterians, who had no interest in humiliating the king, were happy to stop fighting, whereas the Independents were still determined to secure a complete victory and impose their terms on Charles. In the months after Marston Moor, Cromwell bitterly attacked his commander-in-chief the Earl of Manchester for his dithering approach. At the Battle of Newbury, in particular, he felt that Manchester's failure to take positive action had probably cost **Parliament** a decisive final victory.

It was time, Cromwell decided, to get rid of generals like Manchester, who owed

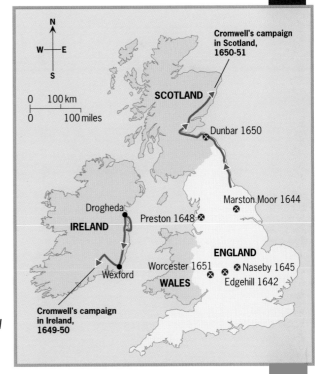

▶ *Major battles of the English Civil War and Cromwell's campaigns in Ireland and Scotland.*

their position to their high social rank, and who sided with the Parliamentary conservatives. In December 1644 he and his supporters introduced the Self-Denying Ordinance, which forced all MPs and peers to resign their army posts. Cromwell tried to resign his own post, but Parliament, knowing that it could not afford to lose such a brilliant military leader, decided to make an exception of him. He was allowed to retain his position as commander of the cavalry.

The New Model Army

In the meantime, Cromwell had pushed ahead with his plans to create a new army on the lines of his own **Ironsides**. The 'New Model Army' was to be 22,000 strong. Unlike previous armies, which had been gathered together when needed, the New Model Army would be a permanent army, paid for by regular taxation. Its soldiers, like Cromwell's original Ironsides, would be men of religion, honest, disciplined and committed to their cause. In fact, for most of the next ten years, the New Model Army would operate as the military arm of the Independents.

Sir Thomas Fairfax was given command of the New Model Army, with Cromwell as his (at first, unofficial) second-in-command. Cromwell swiftly won several minor battles. 'Surely God delights that you have endeavoured to reform your armies,' he wrote to Parliament.

The Battle of Naseby

TO LOCATE NASEBY, SEE THE MAP ON PAGE 25.

The final major battle of the first stage of the war was fought close by the Northamptonshire village of Naseby on 14 June 1645. This time the king was present on the battlefield, although he left the command of his army to his nephew Prince Rupert. On the Parliamentary side, Fairfax

▶ *Thomas Fairfax, the first commander of the New Model Army.*

commanded, with Cromwell in overall charge of the cavalry and the New Model Army's right wing. Henry Ireton, soon to be Cromwell's son-in-law and newly promoted to second-in-command of the cavalry, led the left wing. Before the battle, Cromwell was excited as ever by the prospect of action. 'Riding alone about my business' he later wrote, 'I could not but smile out to God in praises, in assurance of victory.'

The battle began well for the Royalists, with Prince Rupert's cavalry charge from the Royalist right scattering Ireton's horsemen on the Parliamentary left, and the king's **infantry** in the centre pushing back the more-numerous Parliamentary infantry. But, as in other battles, Rupert's horsemen kept going, leaving the battle in headlong pursuit of those they had scattered, and their absence from the battle was soon to prove decisive. On the Parliamentary right, Cromwell's veterans on their heavier horses lumbered into the charge, relying more on weight than speed to break the opposition. And once they had broken the cavalry on the Royalist left, the discipline of the Ironsides enabled Cromwell to wheel them round and direct them, with devastating effect, into the rear of the Royalist infantry. By the time Rupert's cavalry returned to the battlefield, the battle was lost.

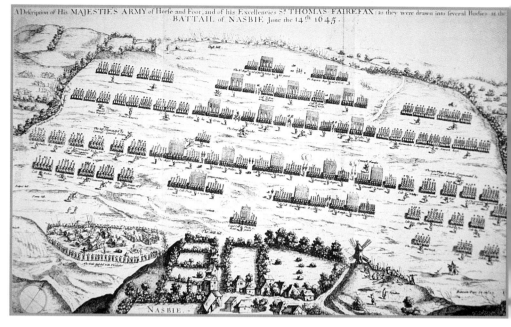

▲ A bird's-eye view of opposing armies at the Battle of Naseby in June 1645, as drawn by an observer.

Rupert and Charles managed to escape, but the war was virtually over. Over the next ten months, minor Royalist strongholds fell one by one as Charles sat powerless in Oxford. In April 1646 he escaped the siege of that city, but had nowhere else to go. In May he gave himself up to the Scots, and they eventually surrendered him to Parliament. The First **Civil War** was over.

A love token

After the Battle of Naseby many Royalist fortresses fell to the Parliamentary forces. During the siege of Bridgewater in Somerset, Mrs Wyndham, the wife of the Royalist commander, fired a cannon at Cromwell, killing the man next to him. She later sent Cromwell a message asking whether he had received her 'love token'.

7 The fall of the king

As long as the king remained unbeaten, the alliance between the **Presbyterians** (who dominated **Parliament**) and the **Independents** (who controlled the New Model Army) had held together, but now that the war was over, the issues that divided the two victorious groups came increasingly to the fore.

Siding with the Army

Early in 1647, the Presbyterian majority in Parliament tried to disband the Army. However, the soldiers were owed large amounts of back pay. Parliament first tried to ignore this fact, and then came up with an offer which was insultingly low.

In May Cromwell travelled to the Army's headquarters at Saffron Walden to talk to the soldiers' representatives. If the authority of Parliament was destroyed, he told them, then 'nothing but confusion can follow'. At the same time, he sympathized with their grievances and recognized the strength of their feelings. Perhaps most important of all, he knew that his own opinions, particularly when it came to religion, were closer to those of the soldiers than to those of the Presbyterian majority in Parliament.

He went back to Westminster to report on his meetings, but on 25 May Parliament ordered the Army to disband. Cromwell took the decision to throw in his lot with the soldiers. On 3 June he left London, only one step ahead of an arrest warrant issued by Parliament, and joined the Army at Newmarket. After fighting a war on behalf of Parliament's right to rule, he was now saying, in effect, that the principles and beliefs he shared with the majority of the Army were more important. He had already given orders for the seizure of the king, who had been held captive at Holmby House in

▲ *London in 1647, as drawn and engraved by Wenceslaus Hollar. In that year the New Model Army occupied the city to intimidate the Presbyterian majority in Parliament.*

Nottinghamshire since February 1647, when the Scots had finally handed him over to Parliament.

Parliament now offered to pay the soldiers all they were owed, but it was too late. The Army responded by demanding the expulsion of certain Presbyterian MPs from Parliament. This was refused, and the MPs in question tried, in late July, to mount an uprising in London. The Army responded by occupying the capital. By early August there was no doubt that Oliver Cromwell, the Army's real leader, had become the single most powerful individual in England.

Opposition from right and left

The occupation of London solved little. The Presbyterians, though temporarily cowed by the Army, would not go away. The problem of how to deal with the king remained. New divisions were becoming apparent in the Army between those, like Cromwell, who wanted a revolution in morals and behaviour – the **Godly reformation** – and others, particularly among the ordinary soldiers, who were now campaigning for a full-scale social and political revolution.

Cromwell and other Army leaders spoke to the king – Cromwell was impressed by Charles' devotion to his children – and offered him a deal called the '**Heads of Proposals**', which left him with the crown and some of his former powers. However, the growing bitterness between Presbyterians and Independents encouraged Charles to be stubborn. He kept playing for time, thinking that his enemies would eventually destroy each other.

Meanwhile, the soldiers' representatives, many of whom now belonged to a group called the Levellers (see page 32), had come up with their own set of proposals for the future of England. Their '**Agreement of the People**' looked forward to a **democratic** republic. Questions of religion would be left to the individual, but a parliament elected by a greatly extended **franchise** would have the final say in most matters.

The Putney Debates

In the autumn of 1647, at St Mary's Church in Putney, Cromwell, Ireton and other Army leaders debated the Heads of Proposals and the Agreement of the People. It became clear that a huge gulf separated the generals, now usually known as the Grandees, from the rank-and-file soldiers. Cromwell himself thought that giving the vote to those without property would threaten the stability of the whole society. He wanted all levels of society to behave in a more moral, God-fearing way, but he had no desire to abolish those levels altogether.

FOR DETAILS ON KEY PEOPLE OF CROMWELL'S TIME, SEE PAGE 58.

The Levellers

The most important group of extreme **radicals** to emerge from the turmoil of the **Civil War** were the Levellers, led by John Lilburne. At first, their main base of support was among the London poor, but by the end of the war they had also won considerable support among the Army's lower ranks.

In a series of documents and pamphlets written between 1647 and 1649 the Leveller leaders outlined their beliefs and demands. They believed that everyone should be treated with equal fairness by the courts, and that everyone should be allowed to follow their own conscience in religious matters. In politics, they believed that the people as a whole should have the final say, not their representatives in Parliament, and certainly not the king. The demands included the abolition of the monarchy, a much wider **franchise** and widespread social reforms. When it became apparent that their demands would not be met, Levellers led mutinies in several Army regiments. These were swiftly suppressed, and over the next few years the movement slowly faded away.

◀ *The Leveller leader John Lilburne behind bars, where he spent much of his adult life.*

The Second Civil War

Power in the Army was finely balanced between the leadership and the ordinary soldiers, and the Putney Debates convinced Cromwell that he must act to reduce the threat posed by the Levellers and their supporters. When one army unit staged an unauthorized meeting a few weeks later, he had the ringleaders arrested and one of them shot. He may also have engineered – or at least turned a blind eye to – the king's escape from captivity in November 1647. If the king were on the loose, and further fighting seemed likely, Cromwell hoped the Army would put aside its disputes with Parliament and concentrate on defeating the king.

The Second Civil War, which lasted from January to August 1648, helped to solve Cromwell's problem with the king. By the time the king's newly raised army had been crushed by Cromwell at the Battle of Preston, the country had once more been thrown into turmoil and many more families had lost loved ones. Most people blamed the king for starting this

TO LOCATE PRESTON, SEE THE MAP ON PAGE 25.

▼ *The Battle of Preston in August 1648, as painted by Charles Cattermole. Cromwell's victory in this battle brought the Second Civil War to an end.*

second war, and the number of those willing to see him pay for his crimes rose accordingly. When the Presbyterians in Parliament refused to vote for a trial, Army troops under Colonel Thomas Pride expelled them. Cromwell was still in the North with the bulk of the Army, but he announced his approval of **Pride's Purge**. He was now certain that England would never have peace while Charles was alive.

From monarchy to Commonwealth

Returning to London, Cromwell poured all his energies into organizing the king's trial. He bullied reluctant lawyers and MPs into attendance, and, when the king was found guilty, he persuaded and threatened 55 prominent men to join him in signing the death warrant. On 30 January 1649 the axe descended on Charles' neck, and England became a republic known as 'the Commonwealth'. For the first and last time in British history a monarch had been executed by the representatives of the people. Cromwell himself is said to have been at prayer during the execution. He never expressed any regrets. For him, the king's death had become a necessary step on the road to the **Godly reformation**.

▼ *The warrant for the king's execution. Cromwell's signature and seal are the third in the left-hand column.*

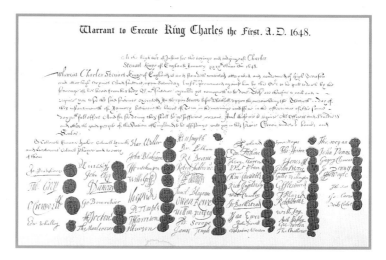

▲ The beheading of the king outside the Whitehall Banqueting Hall. Portraits of Fairfax, Charles and Cromwell line the top of this German print of the time.

After the execution of the king, the monarchy and the **House of Lords** were abolished as being 'useless, burdensome and dangerous'. This left Parliament with only one chamber, the **House of Commons**. Elections were not held, leaving those MPs who had survived Pride's Purge in control of what became known as the 'Rump Parliament'. The Rump appointed a Council of State comprising 40 members to govern the country until a permanent new **constitution** could be agreed. Cromwell became its first chairman.

A new political system would obviously take some time to set up, and there were other, more urgent matters demanding Cromwell's and the new government's attention. The most serious of these was rebellion in Ireland.

Ireland and Scotland

The Irish rebellion, which had broken out in 1641, had never been defeated, because neither Charles nor his opponents had ever trusted the other with an army to do so. By 1649 it had spread to include not only Irish **Roman Catholic** opposition to English rule but also Royalist English settlers who refused to recognize the new Commonwealth. Not surprisingly, many in London feared that the dead king's son, another Charles, might choose to use Ireland as the springboard for a Royalist comeback. Parliament's rule over the island had to be re-established, and quickly.

Ireland

In the spring and early summer of 1649 Cromwell organized his forces for the expedition, taking great care to ensure that his troops were loyal. On the one hand, he made sure that they were well-trained, well-fed and well-paid; on the other, he stamped down hard on any Leveller dissent.

To locate Drogheda, see the map on page 25.

He crossed over to Ireland in the summer, and laid siege to the walled town of Drogheda, north of Dublin, in September.

▼ *The storming of Drogheda in September 1649. The massacre of civilians which followed left a lasting stain on Cromwell's reputation.*

The Royalist commander refused to surrender, and once the walls had been breached no mercy was shown. Almost the entire garrison of 2,000 men, and a similar number of civilians, were slaughtered. A month later the town of Wexford suffered much the same fate. After an eight-day siege over 3,000 soldiers, priests and civilians were put to the sword.

TO LOCATE WEXFORD, SEE THE MAP ON PAGE 25.

Why were Cromwell and his Army so brutal? Fearing an invasion of England from Scotland or the Continent, Cromwell felt that he had to subdue Ireland as quickly as possible, and hoped that the ruthless treatment of Drogheda and Wexford would encourage others to surrender. He was also taking revenge for the mostly-imaginary atrocities committed by the Irish against the English in 1641.

▶ *Henry Cromwell, who was appointed Lord-Lieutenant of Ireland by his father in 1655.*

Henry and Richard Cromwell

When Cromwell returned from Ireland his sons Richard and Henry were 25 and 23 respectively. It seems probable that he originally intended them to live private lives, but the capable Henry persuaded his father to leave him in charge of reconquered Ireland, where he helped to heal some of the wounds left by the recent conflict. His older brother Richard was a weaker, gentler man, with little drive and no apparent ambition, who both mystified and worried his father. He seems to have been thoroughly unsuited to public office, and many were surprised when Cromwell named him, rather than Henry, as his successor in 1657.

Cromwell had no time for Roman Catholics or the Irish. He believed that Catholics were sinners, and like most Englishmen of his time, he thought the Irish were little better than animals and therefore the normal rules no longer applied. His ruthlessness worked in the short term – Ireland was back under English control by the spring of 1650.

Scotland

In June 1650 Cromwell returned to England in triumph, only to find a new threat looming in Scotland. Two months earlier, the dead king's son had been proclaimed Charles II of England, Scotland and Ireland, and in return for his support of their **Presbyterian** Church, the Scots had offered him military help to reclaim his English throne. The Council of State in London had decided to send an army against them, but Fairfax had refused the job of commanding it. Cromwell accepted.

TO LOCATE DUNBAR, SEE THE MAP ON PAGE 25.

On 3 September he brought the Scots to battle at Dunbar, and despite being heavily outnumbered won a great victory. As usual, Cromwell took the victory as proof that he was doing the Lord's work, and as further encouragement to push ahead with the **Godly reformation**. 'Curb the proud and the insolent,' he wrote sternly to Parliament in the aftermath of the battle; 'relieve the oppressed, hear the groans of poor prisoners in England; be pleased to reform the abuses of all professions, and if there be anyone that makes many poor to make a few rich, that suits not a Commonwealth.'

The victory at Dunbar was not the end of the campaign, however, and Charles II was actually crowned at Scone early in 1651. Cromwell was ill for much of the winter – probably with a recurrence of the malaria (a fever transmitted by mosquitos) which he had caught in Ireland – but was back in the saddle by the spring. Forcing the would-be king and his army south into England, he gave chase, and finally caught up with them at Worcester. There on 3 September, a year to the day after the Battle of Dunbar, Cromwell fought and won the last great battle of the British **civil wars**. Charles escaped to France, but the Royalist cause was lost for the foreseeable future.

TO LOCATE WORCESTER, SEE THE MAP ON PAGE 25.

It was now almost three years since the old king's execution. It was time, at last, to heal the wounds, and to begin the Godly reformation of England.

▲ Cromwell at the Battle of Dunbar in September 1650, as painted, over two hundred years later, by A. C. Gow.

The Commonwealth

In the autumn of 1651, Cromwell had two ambitions for England. The first was a lasting political settlement. The second was his programme of social and religious reforms – the **Godly reformation**.

Unfortunately for Cromwell, these two ambitions were mutually exclusive. While a political settlement required agreement on how the country was to be governed, social and religious changes were bound to be divisive, because some wanted to slow reform down, others to speed it up. Cromwell was the most powerful man in England, but for the remaining seven years of his life he would always be under attack from one side or the other, and often from both. Unable to please everyone, he would end up pleasing hardly anyone.

The Rump

The Long **Parliament** – now known as the Rump Parliament – had been elected in 1640. Many of the more conservative MPs who had left

◀ A sarcastic view of Cromwell's England: the devil drives his carriage across the king's body while Cromwell holds liberty and the church at the point of his sword.

around the time of the king's execution, had returned. The Rump as a whole was now reluctant to introduce the reforms for which many believed the war had been fought. When urged by Cromwell and the Council of State to do so, it either refused or simply played for time.

The Levellers and other revolutionary groups had lost much of their influence in the Army, but the Army leadership, most of them Grandees like Cromwell himself, were still much more **radical** in outlook than the Rump. They grew increasingly frustrated by the lack of progress in introducing reforms, and in August 1652 issued a Declaration of the Army which demanded early action from Parliament.

Cromwell, caught between the two, tried to persuade the Rump to introduce reforms, but by March 1653 his patience was exhausted. As usual when a difficult decision loomed, he took himself away from work, thought the matter through, and then returned, his mind made up, to take drastic action. On 20 April he invaded the **House of Commons** with his soldiers, told the MPs they were 'corrupt and unjust men and scandalous to the profession of the Gospel [the teachings of Christ]', and expelled them.

The SPEECH

WHICH WAS SPOKEN BY

Oliver Cromwell,

When he diſſolved the Long Parliament.

IT is high Time for Me to put an End to your Sitting in this Place, which you have diſhonoured by your Contempt of all Virtue, and defiled by your Practice of every Vice; Ye are a factious Crew and Enemies to all good Government; Ye are a Pack of mercenary Wretches, and would, like *Eſau*, ſell your Country for a Meſs of Pottage; and, like *Judas*, betray your GOD for a few Pieces of Money: Is there a ſingle Virtue now remaining amongſt you? Is there one Vice you do not poſſeſs? Ye have no more Religion than my Horſe! Gold is your God: Which of you have not bartered your Conſcience for Bribes? Is there a Man amongſt you that has the leaſt Care for the Good of the Common-Wealth? Ye ſordid Proſtitutes, Have you not defiled this Sacred Place, and turned the LORD's Temple into a Den of Thieves, by your immoral Principles and wicked Practices? Ye are grown intolerably odious to the whole Nation; You were deputed here to get Grievances redreſſed; Are not yourſelves become the greateſt Grievance? Your Country therefore calls upon me to cleanſe this Augean Stable, by putting a final Period to your iniquitous Procedings in this Houſe;----and which, by God's Help, and the Strength he has given Me, I am now come to do. I command ye, therefore, upon the Peril of your Lives, to depart immediately out of this Place;----Go, get out, make Haſte, ye Venal Slaves, begone! So take away that ſhining Bauble there, and lock up the Doors.

▲ *A report of the fiery and violent attack on MPs which Cromwell delivered to the Rump Parliament on 20 April 1653.*

Barebones

But what was to replace the Rump? Cromwell knew that fresh elections were unlikely to result in a victory for the Grandees, and might well see the return of a **Presbyterian** Parliament. That would mean that his Army had won the war only to lose the peace.

Instead of elections, a new Parliament of 140 members was appointed by Cromwell and his **Council of Officers**. Some were personally known to the selectors, others were suggested by churches up and down the country. The new members were not all **radicals**, but care was taken to ensure that the majority were. One of the new MPs had the particularly unusual name of Praise-be-to-God Barebones, and the Parliament as a whole came to be known as the Barebones Parliament. Cromwell had great hopes for it. 'Truly you are called by God to rule with him and for him,' he told the opening meeting, tears coursing down his cheeks.

In some ways, the Barebones Parliament lived up to his expectations. Unlike the Rump, it certainly worked hard. Civil marriage (marriage without a religious ceremony) and a Registry (official list) of Births, Marriages and Deaths were introduced. Taxes were simplified, and work begun on reforming the legal system. Protection for the mentally ill and greater relief for the poor were both provided, and the punishment of criminals was made more humane. The possible abolition of tithes – a very controversial measure – was discussed at length. All in all, 80 **bills** were introduced and 26 laws passed between July and December 1653.

Tithes

Tithes were taxes which every **parishioner** paid for the maintenance of the local church and the living of the clergy (religious officials). The Presbyterians, who favoured a single unified church and the conservative, layered society which went with it, were all in favour of tithes. The **Independents**, who favoured a more equal society and had no use for such a church, saw no reason why they should have to pay for one.

But if the Rump had been too conservative for Cromwell, the Barebones Parliament proved too radical. Many of the ideas thrown up by its more revolutionary members deeply worried Cromwell. The more revolutionary ideas the Barebones Parliament came up with, the more difficult it made what Cromwell called the 'healing and settling' of the nation.

'Instrument of Government'

In December 1653 the more moderate members of the Barebones Parliament arranged to reach the chamber early, and voted to dismiss the Parliament before their opponents knew what was going on. They then signed a paper handing back power to Cromwell and the other Army leaders. Cromwell denied knowing that this was about to happen, but few were convinced, particularly when it turned out that the plans for a new system of government had already been drawn up.

FOR DETAILS ON KEY PEOPLE OF CROMWELL'S TIME, SEE PAGE 58.

The new system, called the 'Instrument of Government', was drafted by General John Lambert, Cromwell's right-hand man at the time (Ireton had died in 1651). The country would be ruled by a single man, the Lord Protector (Cromwell). He would be assisted by a hand-picked council of 15, and a single chamber Parliament (the House of Commons) would sit for at least five months every three years. A standing (permanent) Army of 30,000 would be paid for out of yearly taxation. Religious toleration for all **Protestants** would be guaranteed.

In theory, Cromwell and Parliament would share authority under the 'Instrument of Government'. In practice, Lord Protector Cromwell and the Army had now taken joint responsibility for the running of England. The Commonwealth had become the Protectorate.

◀ Cromwell in his later years, as painted by C. de Crayer.

Lord Protector

For the first eight months of 1653 the new Lord Protector and his closest colleagues ruled without the hindrance of a **Parliament**. England, Scotland and Ireland were officially united, the remaining revolutionary elements in the Army demoted or dismissed. Cromwell was keen to broaden the support of his new regime. He restored some of the country **gentry's** powers and tried, with some success, to win the confidence of London's influential business community. Tax collection was made more efficient and money poured into the creation of new, and expansion of old, universities in England, Scotland and Ireland. Attempts were made to reform the clergy: while 'triers' examined all new applicants, 'ejectors' weeded out those priests who were more interested in their own advancement than in spreading the word of God.

Having set what he considered a good example of reforming government, Cromwell called elections to the first Parliament of the Protectorate. **Roman Catholics** and known Royalists were ineligible, and only men with a certain amount of property could vote, but the elections were reasonably fair by the standards of the time. Both conservatives and **radicals** were well represented in the new Parliament.

More disillusionment

In April 1654 Cromwell and his wife moved into the royal family's palace on Whitehall. The many paintings and tapestries that had been removed were brought back, and the Protector and Protectress began living, for the first time, in the style of rulers. Their weekends were often spent at Hampton Court Palace, away from the stresses of government.

Though pleased by their rise in living standards, the couple still clung to the values of simplicity and **thrift** their religion dictated. Elizabeth kept cows in St James's Park for milk and was mocked by Royalist sympathizers for being as careful with money as she always had been.

The new Parliament, meanwhile, was proving yet another disappointment. Both conservatives and radicals were much more interested in criticizing and obstructing the new system than in making it work. The conservatives had no interest in backing further reforms, and the radicals were still incensed by the removal of the Army from Parliament's control. This reminded many of their fight with Charles I over the same issue. When MPs tried to draw up a new **constitution** Cromwell's troops surrounded the building and ejected all those who refused to swear loyalty to the Protectorate. When the minimum five-month period for a Parliament came to an end in January 1655, Cromwell simply dismissed it.

Foreign policy

In foreign policy, Cromwell enjoyed rather more success. In 1651 the Rump Parliament had passed a law that prevented the ships of any other nation from carrying goods into English ports from a third country. This had been aimed at Dutch dominance of sea trade, and war between the two nations had resulted. A series of naval victories by Admiral Blake allowed

House on fire

'If it be my liberty to walk abroad in the fields, or to take a journey, yet it is not my wisdom to do so when my house is on fire.'
(Cromwell, trying to explain to the members of the Protectorate's first Parliament that they were being irresponsible – England needed constructive assistance, not destructive criticism)

▲ One of the naval battles fought during the Anglo-Dutch War of 1652–54, painted by Abraham Beerstraten.

Cromwell to make a favourable peace in early 1654. He then turned his attention to the sort of enemies he preferred – Catholic countries ruled by **absolute monarchs**, like Spain.

Cromwell was keen to take advantage of the trade and settlement possibilities opening up in the Americas, and in December 1654 he dispatched an expedition to the islands of the Caribbean Sea. Its original aim was to seize the island of Hispaniola (now Haiti and the Dominican Republic) from Spain, but it suffered a naval defeat early in April 1655. Making the best of a bad situation, the British force seized the lesser prize of the island of Jamaica instead.

This was disappointing, but a start had been made. Throughout the period of the Protectorate, Cromwell made great efforts to expand the Navy, and over 200 ships were built between 1655 and 1660. Many historians have argued that Cromwell's strengthening of British sea power laid the foundations for the future British Empire.

The Major-Generals

The coincidence, early in 1655, of naval defeat at the hands of Spain and a Royalist uprising in the West Country convinced Cromwell that God was unhappy with the condition of England. He decided to tighten his control over the country's regions, and at the same time to set higher standards of behaviour for ordinary people.

From August, England was divided into 11 regions, each of which was administered by a Major-General commanding 500 troops. These enforced, with varying degrees of strictness, the existing laws against drunkenness, blasphemy (mocking of religious beliefs), swearing and other anti-religious behaviour. Theatres were closed, gambling forbidden, and singing and dancing were heavily curtailed. The Sabbath (Sunday, the Christian religious day of rest) was very strictly observed.

Not surprisingly, the Major-Generals were very unpopular. The local gentry resented their take-over of local law-enforcement, and the mass of the people saw them as 'killjoys'. The upkeep of 500 soldiers was very expensive, and not all the money could be raised by taxing Royalist estates.

King Oliver?

Thirteen months after his appointment of the Major-Generals, Cromwell summoned the Second Parliament of the Protectorate. Like Charles before him, he needed funds to fight a war, in his case the war with Spain that he had

◀ A silver crown coin from the time of the Protectorate bears a portrait of Cromwell.

Refusing the crown

'I am ready to serve not as a king, but as a constable ... a good constable to keep the peace of the parish.'

(Cromwell, refusing the kingship in 1657)

started in the Caribbean. Parliament gave him the money, but also put an end to the Major-Generals by refusing to renew the taxes that paid for them.

Many MPs did not like the high-minded Major-Generals. However, Parliament's own treatment of James Naylor – an early **Quaker**, accused of blasphemy – was even more intolerant. In late 1656, Naylor was branded, bored through the tongue, twice flogged, and then imprisoned for life. After this many people began wondering how far Parliament, unrestrained by a king, might go. Once Cromwell was dead there was the prospect of a supremely powerful Parliament.

One alternative to an all-powerful Parliament was a stronger Lord Protector. In March 1657 a large number of MPs presented Cromwell with a plan for a new constitution – the 'Humble Petition and Advice'. This went further than the 'Instrument of Government', offering him the kingship, the right to choose his successor, and the right to choose a second house of Parliament. It was a return to the old constitution, with Cromwell enjoying similar powers to those once enjoyed by Charles I.

Cromwell accepted the new powers but refused the kingship. He knew the Army would oppose it, that acceptance might set off another **civil war**. He must also have asked himself what all the bloodletting and turmoil had been for, if the end

Forms of government 1640–58
The Monarchy (1640–49)
The Short Parliament (April–May 1640)
The Long Parliament (November 1640–December 1648)
The Rump of the Long Parliament (December 1648–
January 1649)

The Commonwealth (1649–53)
The Rump of the Long Parliament (January 1649–April 1653)
Barebones Parliament (July–December 1653)

The Protectorate (1653–60)
First Parliament (September 1654–January 1655)
Major-Generals (August 1655–September 1656)
Second Parliament (first session, September 1656–May 1657)
Second Parliament (second session, January–February 1658)

result was only to exchange one king for another. Cromwell was ambitious for his country and driven by his religion, but he had never been driven by personal ambition.

Death
In any event, his life was drawing to a close. There was time, in 1658, for the summoning and dismissal of one more Parliament, but his health, never perfect since the Irish expedition, was failing. His favourite daughter Betty was in even worse straits, and Cromwell watched over her, trying hard not to show his distress, as she died slowly and painfully of cancer that summer. A month after her death, on 3 September, the anniversary of his victories at Dunbar and Worcester, he himself died. He was 59 years old.

Cromwell had chosen his elder surviving son Richard to succeed him, but of all his sons, Richard was the least capable of ruling a country. After failing to gain the wholehearted support of either Parliament or the Army he effectively retired from political life. The Army leaders then fell out with each other, and by the spring of 1660 Parliament had negotiated the restoration (bringing back) of the monarchy and invited Charles II home.

The new king took revenge on his father's executioners. The bodies of Oliver Cromwell, Henry Ireton and John Bradshaw, who had presided over Charles I's trial, were dug up, dragged around the streets of London and decapitated. Their heads were then hung on poles above Westminster Hall, where they remained for many years.

▼ *After his death, Cromwell lies in state at London's Somerset House.*

There is no doubting Oliver Cromwell's enormous influence on events in Britain during his own lifetime. In the late 1630s he became a significant figure in his own area of East Anglia, in the early 1640s a figure of national importance through **Parliament's** challenge to the king and the slide into **civil war**. During the first difficult years of that war he played an increasingly important role, first as an organizer of the Parliamentary forces, and then as a brave, energetic and imaginative cavalry commander. His contribution to the victory at Marston Moor was vital, and from that moment on, through the last 14 years of his life, he became the single most influential figure in British politics and life.

Soldier and politician

Cromwell's reputation as a soldier remains high. Like any great military tactician, he made the most of the weaponry available in his time, honing the use of cavalry to a disciplined perfection. Time and again, his **Ironsides** proved the decisive element in battles against the Royalist armies. He forged a regiment, and then an army, based on professionalism and belief in a cause. The New Model Army was one of the first modern armies – perhaps the very first – and Cromwell was its principal creator.

His reputation as a politician is less certain. On the plus side, he brought England peacefully through the post-war period, fighting off demands for a return to the past from one side, and demands for a social revolution from the other. He consistently encouraged and organized financial support for education and the arts, and at least began the overdue reform of England's **penal system**. On the minus side, he failed to secure a political settlement, trying and failing with five different forms of government. Most disappointingly for

A believer in truth

'Mr Lely, I desire you would use all your skill to paint my picture truly like me, and not flatter me at all; but remark all these roughnesses, pimples, warts and everything as you see me; otherwise I will never pay a farthing for it.'

(Cromwell, telling the painter Peter Lely not to follow the usual custom of producing a flattering portrait. This was the origin of the phrase 'warts and all', meaning a complete and honest picture.)

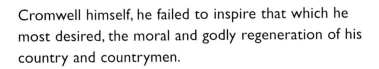

▶ *Cromwell, as painted by Sir Peter Lely.*

Cromwell himself, he failed to inspire that which he most desired, the moral and godly regeneration of his country and countrymen.

For Parliament and business

By the mid-1660s it must, sometimes, have been hard to believe that Cromwell's God-fearing republic had ever existed. The lower classes were back in their places, the bishops were running an intolerant Church of England, and Parliament was again controlled by an alliance of the **gentry** and businessmen. The throne was occupied by a king notorious for his sexual appetites. It was as if Cromwell had left no lasting legacy.

This was a false impression. The monarchy survived, but it was never as powerful again. Nor was the **aristocracy**. Parliament, and the business interests that controlled it, held the upper hand from this point forward. The way had been opened for British **capitalism** to develop, and Cromwell's expansion of British naval power helped it to spread around the world.

The glories and disgraces of the British Empire that followed can thus be partly laid at Cromwell's door. Nowhere was this more obvious than in Ireland, where he left a seemingly permanent legacy of religious hatred. It has been argued that his actions were not particularly harsh for the time, but the real comparison must be with his military behaviour in England and Scotland, which was always far better. Cromwell had every reason to be ashamed of his actions in Ireland.

Reluctant champion

Perhaps Cromwell's greatest contribution to the future of Britain was his support of **democracy** in its widest sense. Certainly he argued against a drastic widening of the **franchise** in the Putney Debates, and during his years in power he often acted against the lower classes. He ordered the shooting of Leveller mutineers, changed his mind about tithes, even supported those whom he had once opposed over the drainage of the Fens. When

◀ *A cartoon from 1657, showing Cromwell 'at war' with Scotland (under his foot), France (under his arm), Ireland (between his legs) and Holland (on the table).*

▲ *The statue of Oliver Cromwell which stands today outside London's Palace of Westminster.*

it came to a clash between political rights and the interests of property, Cromwell almost always chose property.

But that is not the end of the story. Cromwell's experience as a **yeoman** farmer and a soldier brought him into contact with the hopes and fears of ordinary Englishmen, and turned him into a champion – admittedly, a flawed and reluctant one – of the common man. This showed in his promotion of merit over social rank in the New Model Army, his encouragement of education, his desire to make law cheaper and more accessible, his affection for and tolerance of the more **radical** religious sects of his day. Oliver Cromwell is remembered by many as the man who won a war, killed a king, and cut short a revolution, but he should also be remembered as a tireless opponent of unearned privilege.

Timeline

1599	(25 April) Oliver Cromwell is born in Huntingdon.
1616–17	Studies at Sidney Sussex College, Cambridge.
1617	Death of his father.
1620	Marries Elizabeth Bourchier.
1621	Birth of son Robert.
1623	Birth of son Oliver.
1624	Birth of daughter Bridget.
1626	Birth of son Richard.
1628	Elected MP for Huntingdon. Birth of son Henry.
1629	Makes maiden speech in Parliament. Birth of daughter Elizabeth (Betty).
1630	Called before the Privy Council after political quarrel in Huntingdon.
1631	Leaves Huntingdon for St Ives. Birth and death of son James.
1636	Moves to Ely after receiving inheritance.
1636–38	Gets involved in dispute over drainage of the Fens.
1637	Birth of daughter Mary.
1638	Birth of daughter Frances.
1639	Death of eldest son Robert.
1640	Elected MP for Cambridge to both Short and Long Parliaments.
1641	Irish rebellion begins. Grand Remonstrance presented to the king.
1642	King Charles I tries to arrest Parliamentary leaders. Cromwell raises troops in Cambridgeshire and ambushes Royalist convoy. Start of First Civil War. Battle of Edgehill.
1643	Cromwell's cavalry troop becomes a regiment. Cromwell involved in battles at Grantham, Gainsborough and Winceby.
1644	Cromwell promoted to Lieutenant-General. Death of son Oliver. Battle of Marston Moor. Cromwell proposes Self-Denying Ordinance.

1645	Formation of New Model Army. Battle of Naseby.
1646	End of First Civil War.
1647	Cromwell sides with Army against Parliament and has his troops seize the king. Army occupies London. Putney Debates. King escapes.
1648	Second Civil War. Battle of Preston. Pride's Purge.
1649	Trial and execution of King Charles I. Suppression of Leveller mutiny at Burford. Cromwell arrives in Ireland. Orders massacres at Drogheda and Wexford. Returns to England and leaves for Scotland. Battle of Dunbar.
1651	Battle of Worcester ends British civil wars.
1652–54	War with Dutch.
1653	Cromwell dissolves the Rump Parliament. Barebones Parliament. Cromwell accepts 'Instrument of Government' and becomes Lord Protector.
1654–55	First Protectorate Parliament.
1655	Royalist rising in West Country. Cromwell's expeditionary force fails to take Hispaniola. Major-Generals appointed.
1656–57	First session of Second Protectorate Parliament.
1657	Cromwell abandons 'Instrument of Government' and Major-Generals. Is offered the kingship in 'Humble Petition and Advice'. Cromwell rejects kingship but accepts 'Humble Petition and Advice'.
1658	Second session of Second Protectorate Parliament. Death of Cromwell's favourite daughter Betty. Cromwell names son Richard as his successor. Death of Cromwell.
1660	Restoration of monarchy.

Key people of Cromwell's time

Charles I (1600–49). Became king of England in 1625. For most of his first 15 years on the throne he ruled without a **Parliament**, but in 1640 he was forced to call one in order to raise money for his wars with Scotland. Deep disagreements over both religious and **constitutional** matters saw the breach between king and Parliament widen into a **civil war**. After his military defeat in 1646, Charles tried to make the most of divisions between the victors, and eventually managed to spark a second civil war, which he also lost. His opponents tried and executed him in January 1649.

Fairfax, Thomas (1612–71). A **Puritan** and member of the Yorkshire **gentry**. In 1642 he raised troops for the Parliamentary cause in Yorkshire, and won several important victories there and in eastern England. He commanded the Parliamentary army at Marston Moor and Naseby, and was the first Commander-in-Chief of the New Model Army. He refused to play any part in the trial of the king, and turned down command of the invasion of Scotland in 1650.

Hampden, John (1594–1643). Sat in every Parliament from 1621 to his death. He was an outspoken opponent of what he considered Charles I's illegal taxes, and became a national figure over his refusal to pay Ship Money in 1637–38. In the Short and Long Parliaments he was considered second only to Pym as a Parliamentary leader. Once war broke out he raised a regiment from his local county, Buckinghamshire, and was mortally wounded in a skirmish in the summer of 1643.

Ireton, Henry (1611–51). A Parliamentary commander who fought at Edgehill and Newbury, and became one of Cromwell's most trusted lieutenants, marrying his daughter Bridget in 1646. Ireton was mainly responsible for many of the Army's policy proposals in the post-war period, including the '**Heads of Proposals**' scheme for a political settlement which included the king. He went to Ireland with Cromwell, but died of a fever in 1651, aged only 40.

Lambert, John (1619–83). Commanded cavalry under Fairfax in the First Civil War and served Cromwell with distinction in both the Second Civil War and the war with Scotland. He was largely responsible for the 'Instrument of Government' which created the Protectorate and secured the Army generals' position as the most influential group in the country. He served as one of Cromwell's Major-Generals, but fell out with him over his acceptance of the 'Humble Petition and Advice', and was stripped of all his posts. In 1659 he returned to power, but his attempt to save the Protectorate from the Restoration failed and he spent the last 23 years of his life in captivity.

Lilburne, John (1614–57). First imprisoned in the late 1630s for distributing illegal pamphlets attacking the bishops. During the civil war he rose to the rank of Lieutenant-Colonel in the Eastern Association army. After the war he became the most prominent leader of the revolutionary Levellers, and fell out with Cromwell, whom he believed had betrayed the ordinary English people. After the execution of Charles I, he denounced the Commonwealth and tried to incite mutinies in the Army. He was sent into exile in December 1651, later returning to years of captivity.

Pym, John (1584–1643). Entered Parliament in 1614. He became convinced that Charles I was trying to roll back the **Protestant Reformation** in England, and became his committed opponent. He was the leading force for change in the Long Parliament and the driving spirit behind the Grand Remonstrance. In 1643 he took two crucial steps to strengthen the Parliamentary cause, introducing taxes to pay for the war and persuading MPs to sign an alliance with the Scots.

Further reading & other resources

Further reading
Cavaliers and Roundheads, Stewart Ross, Batsford, 1994
Charles I & Oliver Cromwell, John Guy, Ticktock Publishing, 1998
Charles I and the Civil War, Bob Fowke, Hodder, 2001
Cromwell, Jessica Saraga, Batsford, 1999
Edmund Ludlow and the English Civil War, ed. Jane Shuter,
    Heinemann Library, 1994
The Stuarts, Andrew Langley, Heinemann Library, 1997

Places to visit
The Cromwell Museum: Grammar School Walk, Huntingdon

Sources
Battles of the English Civil War, Austin Woolrych, Pan, 1961
Cromwell, Barry Coward, Longman, 1991
Cromwell, Our Chief of Men, Antonia Fraser, Panther, 1975
God's Englishman, Christopher Hill, Penguin, 2000
The King's Peace 1637-41/The King's War 1641-47,
    C.V. Wedgewood, Fontana, 1966
Regicide and Republic, Graham Seel, Cambridge University
    Press, 2001

Websites
The Cromwell Association:
    www.cromwell.argonet.co.uk
The English Civil War Society:
    www.english-civil-war-society.org

Glossary

absolute monarch monarch (whether king or queen, emperor or empress, etc) who has no co-rulers or institutions (like a Parliament, for example) to restrain him or her from doing whatever he or she wants to do

Agreement of the People proposals drawn up by the more radical elements of the Army in reply to the Army Council's Heads of Proposals. They included an end to the monarchy and a huge increase in the number of those entitled to vote.

aristocracy those who have inherited membership of the ruling elite

apprentices people who attach themselves to an employer for a period of time in order to learn a skill or craft

bills (in Parliament) the draft of a proposed new measure or law

capitalism economic system based on private wealth and profit-making

civil war war between different groups in one country

constitution in politics, the way the government of a country, and the institutions which do the governing, are organized

Council of Officers ruling group of Army officers during the Commonwealth and Protectorate

democratic reflecting the wishes of all those involved

divine right to rule belief that an individual, having been given their power to rule by God, was, in the last resort, only answerable to God, and not to the people he or she ruled

(the) establishment those in political and economic control of a society at any particular time

Fifth Monarchists extreme Protestant sect which believed that the 'Fifth Monarchy' – that of Christ – would soon begin, and that their task was to purify the morals of the current society

franchise right to vote. In Cromwell's time only a limited group of landowners, and no women, could vote.

gentry class just below the aristocracy, traditionally divided into four groups: baronets, knights, esquires and gentlemen. In the 17th century about half of England's landed wealth was owned by the gentry.

Godly reformation complete transformation of society according to basic Christian principles (as defined by the Puritans)

Heads of Proposals proposals put by the Army Council to the king in 1647, which included the continuation of the king's veto, the survival of the bishops, two-yearly Parliaments, and Parliamentary control of the armed forces for ten years. The king rejected them out of hand.

House of Commons lower house of the British Parliament. Its members have traditionally been elected, though originally by a very small proportion of the population

House of Lords upper house of the British Parliament. Its members have traditionally been appointed rather than elected, originally by the monarch, and more recently by the elected government.

Independents those Puritans who rejected the church authorities and wished to push the Reformation still further

infantry soldiers who travel and fight on foot

Inns of Court place where barristers (top lawyers) are trained

intermediary go-between

Ironsides nickname given to Cromwell's cavalry

Justice of the Peace person administering the law locally

Norman person from, or with ancestors from, the region of Normandy in northern France. Many Normans settled in Britain after the 'Norman Conquest' of 1066.

parishioner someone who lives in a parish, the area served by a particular church

Parliament in the UK, the law-making body of elected representatives.

penal system way society organizes the punishment of crime

Presbyterians those Puritans who believed in electing their church authorities, and who opposed any further reformation of the Protestant church

Pride's Purge forcible ejection of 231 MPs from Parliament on 6–7 December 1648, carried out by soldiers under the command of Colonel Thomas Pride

Protestantism the form of Christianity which split off from the established church in the 16th-century Reformation

Puritans those who wished to further the 16th-century Reformation by weakening the church authorities and strengthening the individual's direct relationship with God

Quakers radical religious sect that appeared in 1650s England. Quakers rejected formal church services, tithes and authority in general. In later centuries they became well-known for their commitment to peace.

radical (noun) someone who favours fundamental changes in society

radical (adjective) innovative and progressive

Reformation 16th-century movement for reform in the Christian church which ended in the establishment of the Protestant church

Roman Catholic belonging to a Christian church which recognizes the leadership of the Pope. Protestantism split off from Roman Catholicism in the Reformation.

silver plate cups, cutlery, etc plated with silver

sovereignty supreme power

status quo current situation

thrift being careful with money

veto right to reject something

yeomanry class of small independent farmers and tenant farmers

Index

Agreement of the People 31

Barebones Parliament 42–43
Barebones, Praise-be-to-God 42
Beard, Sir Thomas 7, 8
Bourchier, Elizabeth see Cromwell,
   Elizabeth (wife)
Bradshaw, John 51
Bridgewater, siege of 28

Cavaliers 21
Charles I, King 11, 12, 14, 15–16, 19, 28, 31
   execution 34–35
Charles II, King 38–39, 51
Civil War
   First 19–28
   Second 33–34
Commonwealth 34, 40–44
Cromwell, Bridget 22
Cromwell, Elizabeth (mother) 6, 7
Cromwell, Elizabeth (wife) 8–9, 10
Cromwell, Henry 37
Cromwell, Oliver
   death 50–51
   early life and education 6–8
   expansion of Navy 47, 54
   legacy 52–55
   Lord Protector 44–50
   as military leader 19, 20–24, 25–28,
     36–39, 52
   as MP 11, 14, 15, 16, 19, 20, 23
   religious beliefs 7, 13, 29, 38, 45–46
Cromwell, Richard 37, 51
Cromwell, Robert 6, 7

Drogheda, siege of 36, 37
Dunbar, Battle of 38, 39

Edgehill, Battle of 20
Ely 13, 22
Essex, Earl of 19

Fairfax, Thomas 17, 21, 24, 26–27, 35, 38

Gainsborough, siege of 21
Godly reformation 9, 14, 16, 31, 34, 38, 39,
   40
Grand Remonstrance 17
Grandees 31, 41, 42
Grantham 21

Hampden, John 15, 18, 22
Haslerig, Sir Arthur 18
Heads of Proposals 31

Holland, war with 46–47
Holles, Denzil 18
Humble Petition and Advice 49
Huntingdon 6, 7, 8–9, 11

Independents 23, 25, 29, 31
Instrument of Government 43–44
Ireton, Henry 22, 27, 31, 51
Irish rebellion 36–37, 54
Ironsides 20, 26, 52

Lambert, John 44
Levellers 31, 32, 33, 36, 41
Lilburne, John 32
Long Parliament 16, 40–41
'Lord of the Fens' 13

Major-Generals 48–49
Manchester, Earl of 20, 22, 24, 25–26
Marston Moor, Battle of 24, 52

Naseby, Battle of 26–27, 28
Navy, expansion of 47, 54
Naylor, James 49
New Model Army 26–27, 52, 55
Newbury, Battle of 25

Oxford 23, 28

Presbyterians 23, 25, 29, 30, 31, 34
Preston, Battle of 33
Pride, Thomas 34
Pride's Purge 34
Protectorate 44–50
Puritans 7, 8, 9, 12, 13, 22, 23
Putney Debates 31, 33, 54
Pym, John 12, 18, 22

Reformation 9, 12
restoration of the monarchy 51
Roundheads 21
Rump Parliament 35, 40–41
Rupert, Prince 24, 26, 27–28

St Ives 11
Scotland, war in 38–39
Self-Denying Ordinance 26
Short Parliament 16
Spain, war with 47, 48–49
Strode, William 18

Wexford, siege of 37
Winceby, Battle of 21
Worcester, Battle of 39

York 24